Tumbleweed Tom
on the Texas Trail

by Jackie Hopkins
Illustrated by Kay Salem

This book is dedicated to the teachers and librarians of Texas. — JH

I would like to thank my friends at Neverending Tales Bookstore for their never ending support and encouragement. I would also like to thank Doris Duncombe and Katherine Keller who saw the need and believed in Tumbleweed Tom. Thank you to my husband, Jeff, and my children, Jonathan and Katie. — JH

To my Little Lone Star, Lonna. — KS

Charlesbridge

I'm Tumbleweed Tom,
Come ride for a spell!
I'll take you 'round Texas,
A state I know well.

We'll ride through the south,
The north, east, and west,
Then you can decide
Which part you like best.

Down south in the Valley
We'll start on our ride,
Where the citrus that's grown
Gives Texans great pride.

Our next stop is Brownsville
Where veggies abound.
There is plenty of sunshine
So crops grow year 'round.

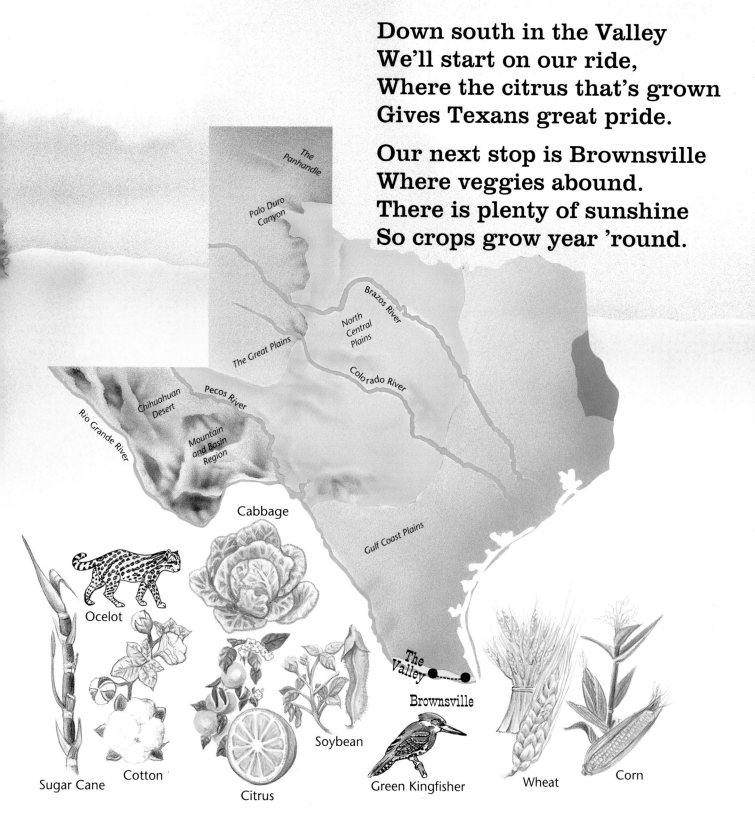

Which is the southernmost city in Texas? Brownsville! People like to spend their vacation in Brownsville because of its subtropical climate. That means the winters are warm and sunny.

Texans call the area at the southern tip of Texas, the Valley. But it really isn't a valley. It's a flat plain that the Rio Grande flows through.

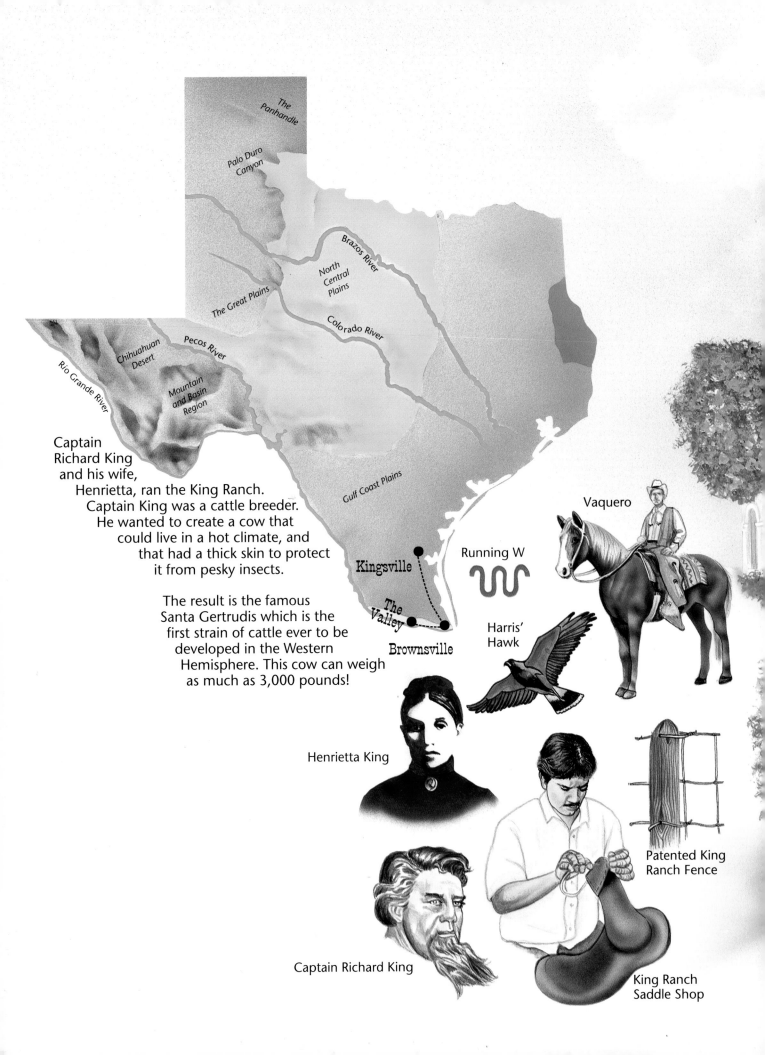

The Panhandle

Palo Duro Canyon

Brazos River

North Central Plains

The Great Plains

Chihuahuan Desert

Pecos River

Colorado River

Rio Grande River

Mountain and Basin Region

Gulf Coast Plains

Kingsville

The Valley

Brownsville

Captain Richard King and his wife, Henrietta, ran the King Ranch. Captain King was a cattle breeder. He wanted to create a cow that could live in a hot climate, and that had a thick skin to protect it from pesky insects.

The result is the famous Santa Gertrudis which is the first strain of cattle ever to be developed in the Western Hemisphere. This cow can weigh as much as 3,000 pounds!

Vaquero

Running W

Harris' Hawk

Henrietta King

Patented King Ranch Fence

Captain Richard King

King Ranch Saddle Shop

In Kingsville we find
A Texas-size spread.
The King Ranch is where
Santa Gertrudis are bred.

At King Ranch we'll watch
Their famous ranch hands.
Here the expert vaquero
Still rides, ropes, and brands.

TUMBLEWEED
TOM

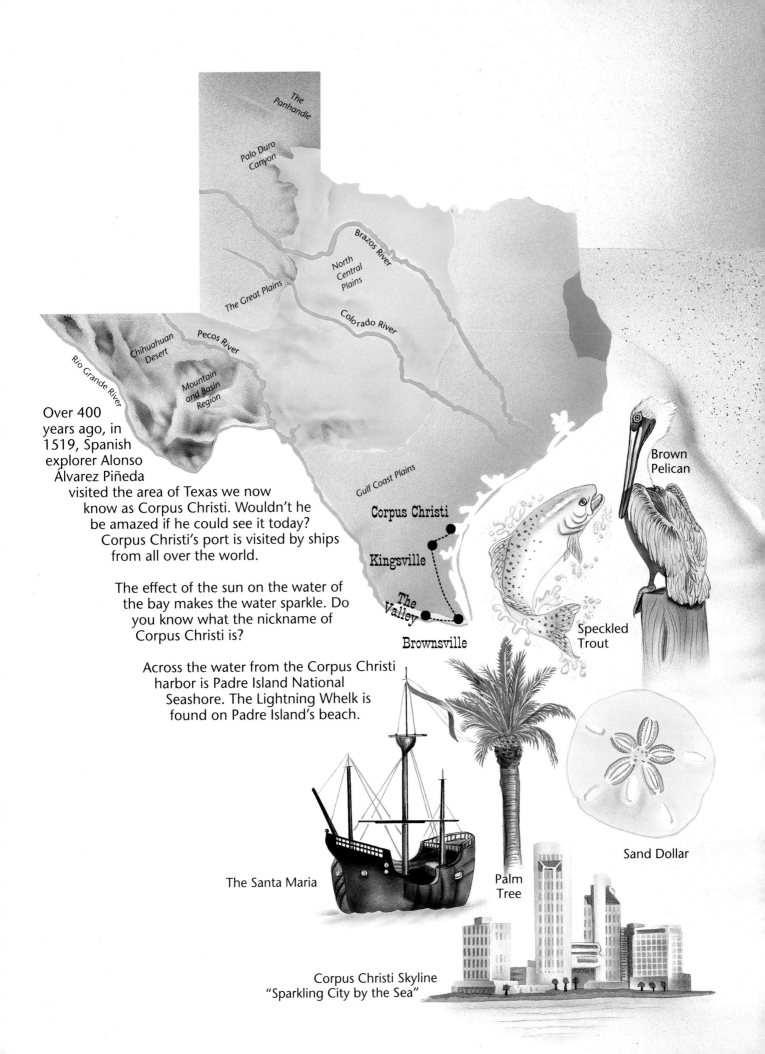

The Panhandle

Palo Duro Canyon

Brazos River

North Central Plains

The Great Plains

Colorado River

Chihuahuan Desert

Pecos River

Rio Grande River

Mountain and Basin Region

Gulf Coast Plains

Corpus Christi

Kingsville

The Valley

Brownsville

Over 400 years ago, in 1519, Spanish explorer Alonso Álvarez Piñeda visited the area of Texas we now know as Corpus Christi. Wouldn't he be amazed if he could see it today? Corpus Christi's port is visited by ships from all over the world.

The effect of the sun on the water of the bay makes the water sparkle. Do you know what the nickname of Corpus Christi is?

Across the water from the Corpus Christi harbor is Padre Island National Seashore. The Lightning Whelk is found on Padre Island's beach.

Brown Pelican

Speckled Trout

Sand Dollar

The Santa Maria

Palm Tree

Corpus Christi Skyline
"Sparkling City by the Sea"

We're near Corpus Christi.
It's not far away.
Here ships come and go
In and out of the bay.

This city sparkles
From the light on the sea.
Look! Lightning Whelk shells
On the beach, one, two, three.

Here in Gonzales
We rebelled and cried, "No!"
To the unfair demands
Of old Mexico.

There is the cannon they
Named, "Come and Take It."
Though the *soldados* sure tried,
They just couldn't make it.

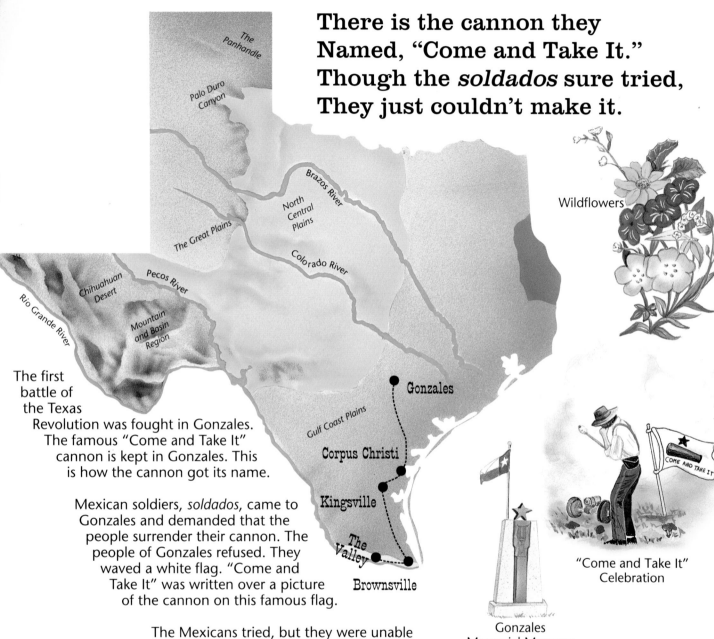

Wildflowers

The first
battle of
the Texas
Revolution was fought in Gonzales.
The famous "Come and Take It"
cannon is kept in Gonzales. This
is how the cannon got its name.

Mexican soldiers, *soldados*, came to
Gonzales and demanded that the
people surrender their cannon. The
people of Gonzales refused. They
waved a white flag. "Come and
Take It" was written over a picture
of the cannon on this famous flag.

The Mexicans tried, but they were unable
to take the cannon away from the brave
soldiers of Gonzales.

"Come and Take It"
Celebration

Gonzales
Memorial Museum

The city of Houston
Is next, follow me.
It's where they keep finding
That black Texas tea!

What, besides oil, do
We find at this place?
NASA, where people
Learn about space.

San Jacinto
Monument

Alabama-Coushatta
Indian

Astronaut

Jean Lafitte

The Panhandle

Palo Duro
Canyon

Brazos River

North
Central
Plains

The Great Plains

Colorado River

Chihuahuan
Desert

Pecos River

Rio Grande River

Mountain
and Basin
Region

Oil
Derrick

Medical
Center

San Jacinto Monument

Houston

Gonzales

Battleship
Texas

35

Gulf Coast Plains

Corpus Christi

The San Jacinto
Monument marks the site of the final
battle of the Texas Revolution. The
Texan soldiers were led by Sam Houston.
During this battle, the Texan soldiers
yelled, "Remember the Alamo!"

Did you know that this monument is so
huge that there is a museum inside the
base of the tower? The star at the top
weighs 220 tons!

Kingsville

Prairie Chicken

The
Valley

Brownsville

Sam Houston

San Jacinto is east,
On this flat coastal plain.
This battleground rang
With that famous refrain:

"Remember the Alamo!"
Was shouted by all.
Here Sam Houston caused
Santa Anna to fall.

The Piney Woods has many species of hardwood pine trees such as the longleaf, pinyon, shortleaf, and loblolly.

This woodland region was once inhabited by the Caddo Indians. The Caddos were unusual among the Native American tribes because women were chosen to be the chief in their tribe.

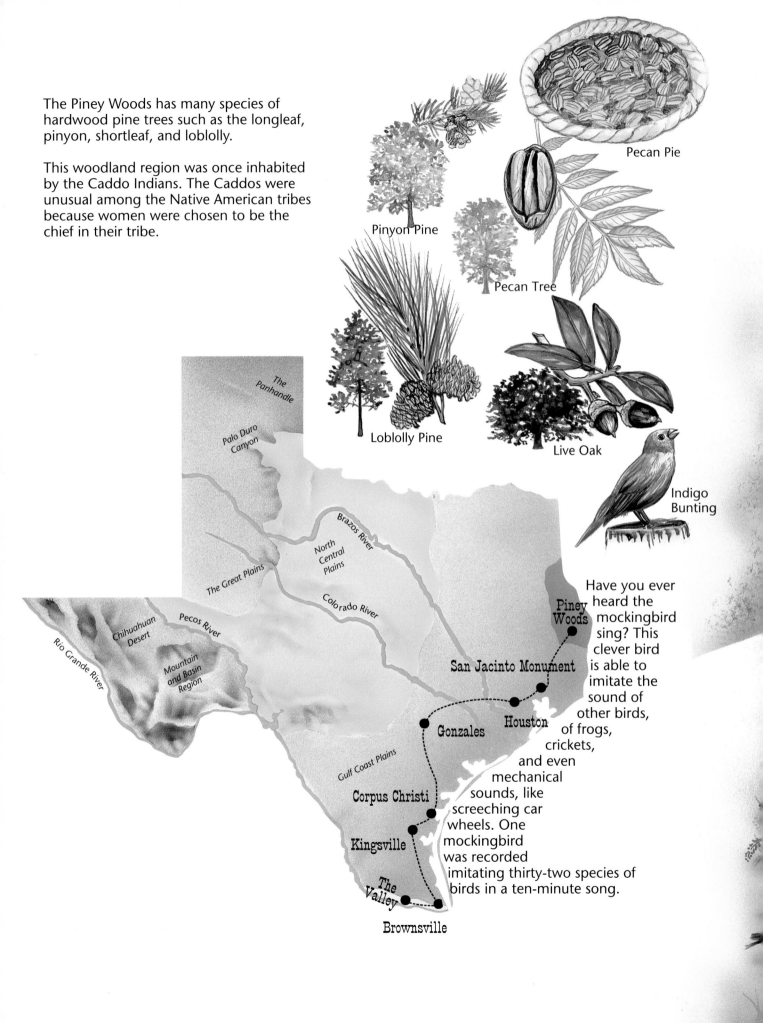

Pecan Pie

Pinyon Pine

Pecan Tree

Loblolly Pine

Live Oak

Indigo Bunting

The Panhandle

Palo Duro Canyon

Brazos River

North Central Plains

The Great Plains

Colorado River

Chihuahuan Desert

Pecos River

Mountain and Basin Region

Río Grande River

Piney Woods

San Jacinto Monument

Gonzales

Houston

Gulf Coast Plains

Corpus Christi

Kingsville

The Valley

Brownsville

Have you ever heard the mockingbird sing? This clever bird is able to imitate the sound of other birds, of frogs, crickets, and even mechanical sounds, like screeching car wheels. One mockingbird was recorded imitating thirty-two species of birds in a ten-minute song.

Let's move to East Texas
With piney woods tall.
Wait...listen closely.
Hear the mockingbird call?

It sounds like six birds.
But it's really just one.
The mockingbird's songs
Are really great fun.

While in these parts,
We'll follow our nose.
In Tyler we find
That sweet yellow rose.

The rose gardens here
Are lovely to see.
And, look over there,
Our state pecan tree!

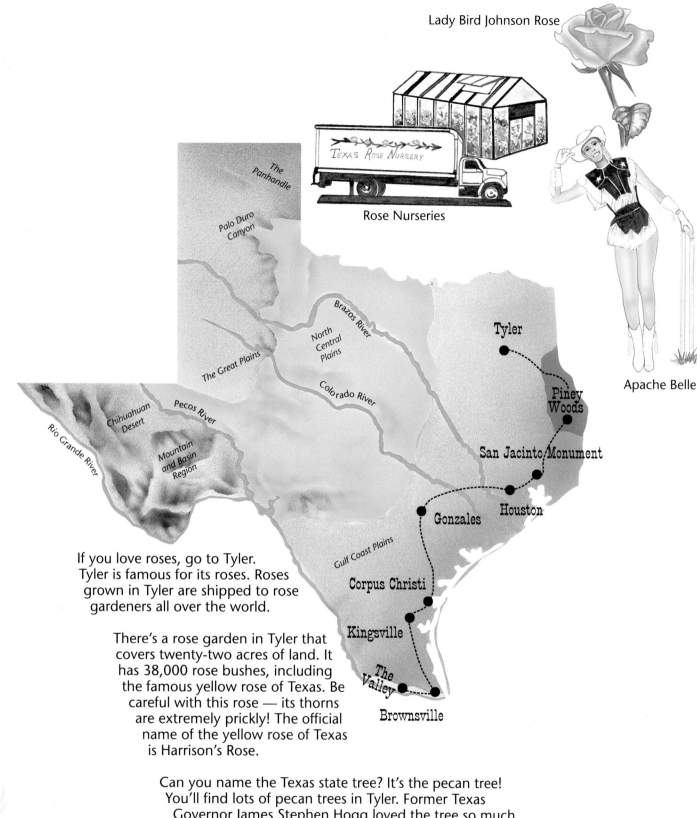

Lady Bird Johnson Rose

Rose Nurseries

Apache Belle

The Panhandle

Palo Duro Canyon

Brazos River

North Central Plains

The Great Plains

Colorado River

Pecos River

Chihuahuan Desert

Rio Grande River

Mountain and Basin Region

Tyler

Piney Woods

San Jacinto Monument

Houston

Gonzales

Gulf Coast Plains

Corpus Christi

Kingsville

The Valley

Brownsville

If you love roses, go to Tyler. Tyler is famous for its roses. Roses grown in Tyler are shipped to rose gardeners all over the world.

There's a rose garden in Tyler that covers twenty-two acres of land. It has 38,000 rose bushes, including the famous yellow rose of Texas. Be careful with this rose — its thorns are extremely prickly! The official name of the yellow rose of Texas is Harrison's Rose.

Can you name the Texas state tree? It's the pecan tree! You'll find lots of pecan trees in Tyler. Former Texas Governor James Stephen Hogg loved the tree so much, he asked that one be planted near his grave. Pecan nuts from this tree are planted all over Texas in his honor.

Our wagon's a-creakin'
Giddy-up, yes siree.
Yonder is Dallas
Known as Big "D."

There's wheelin' and dealin'
And the Texas State Fair.
Look up, it's Big Tex
Saying, "Howdy!" up there.

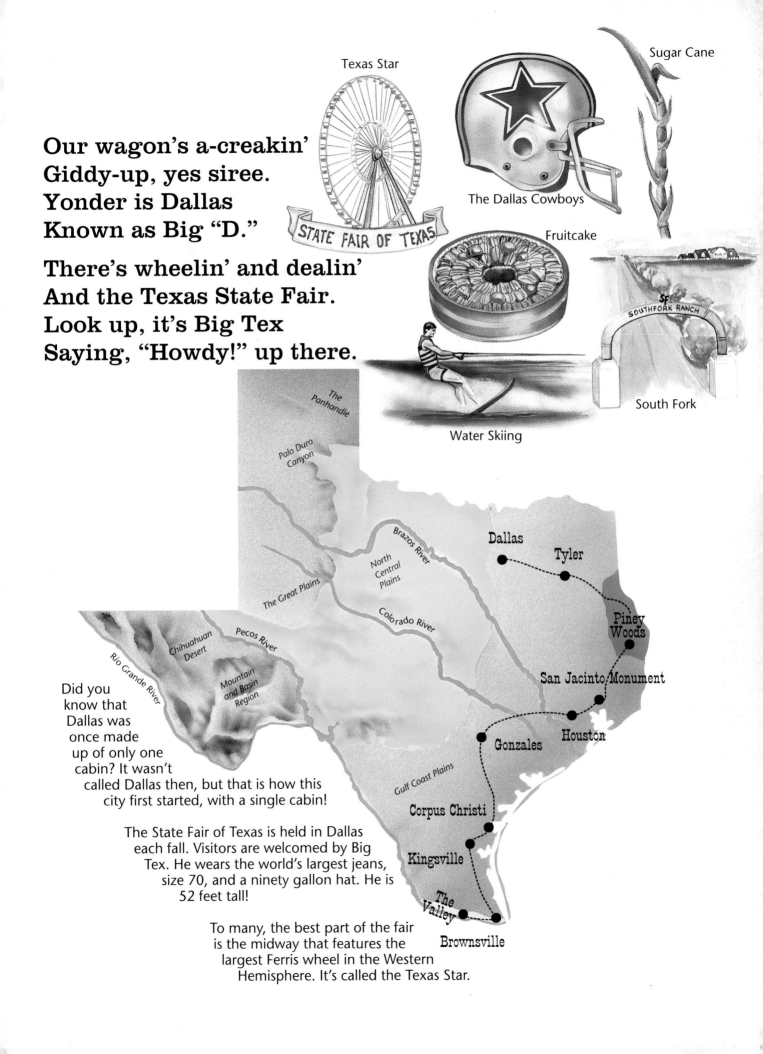

Texas Star

STATE FAIR OF TEXAS

The Dallas Cowboys

Sugar Cane

Fruitcake

South Fork

Water Skiing

The Panhandle

Palo Duro Canyon

Brazos River

North Central Plains

The Great Plains

Colorado River

Chihuahuan Desert

Pecos River

Río Grande River

Mountain and Basin Region

Dallas

Tyler

Piney Woods

San Jacinto Monument

Houston

Gonzales

Gulf Coast Plains

Corpus Christi

Kingsville

The Valley

Brownsville

Did you know that Dallas was once made up of only one cabin? It wasn't called Dallas then, but that is how this city first started, with a single cabin!

The State Fair of Texas is held in Dallas each fall. Visitors are welcomed by Big Tex. He wears the world's largest jeans, size 70, and a ninety gallon hat. He is 52 feet tall!

To many, the best part of the fair is the midway that features the largest Ferris wheel in the Western Hemisphere. It's called the Texas Star.

On these North Central Plains,
Now come hear the tale
Of Fort Worth and cattle
On the Old Chisholm trail.

Here we watch rodeos,
Many each night,
Where cowboys and cowgirls
Compete with delight.

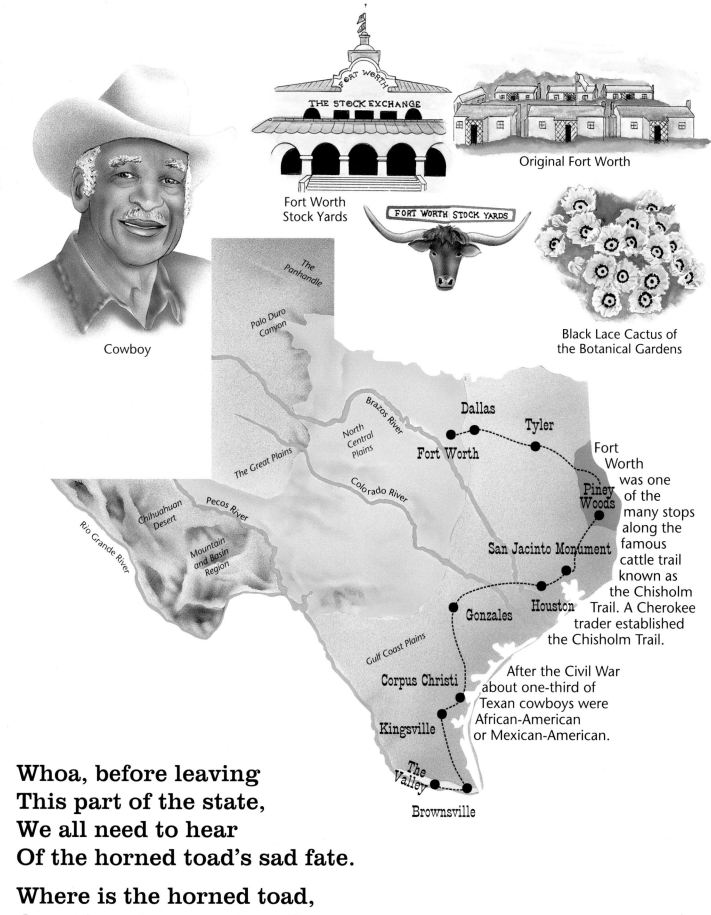

Cowboy

Fort Worth Stock Yards

Original Fort Worth

FORT WORTH STOCK YARDS

Black Lace Cactus of the Botanical Gardens

The Panhandle

Palo Duro Canyon

Brazos River

North Central Plains

The Great Plains

Colorado River

Chihuahuan Desert

Pecos River

Rio Grande River

Mountain and Basin Region

Dallas

Tyler

Fort Worth

Piney Woods

San Jacinto Monument

Houston

Gonzales

Gulf Coast Plains

Corpus Christi

Kingsville

The Valley

Brownsville

Fort Worth was one of the many stops along the famous cattle trail known as the Chisholm Trail. A Cherokee trader established the Chisholm Trail.

After the Civil War about one-third of Texan cowboys were African-American or Mexican-American.

Whoa, before leaving
This part of the state,
We all need to hear
Of the horned toad's sad fate.

Where is the horned toad,
Once found everywhere?
This critter is threatened.
If you see one, take care.

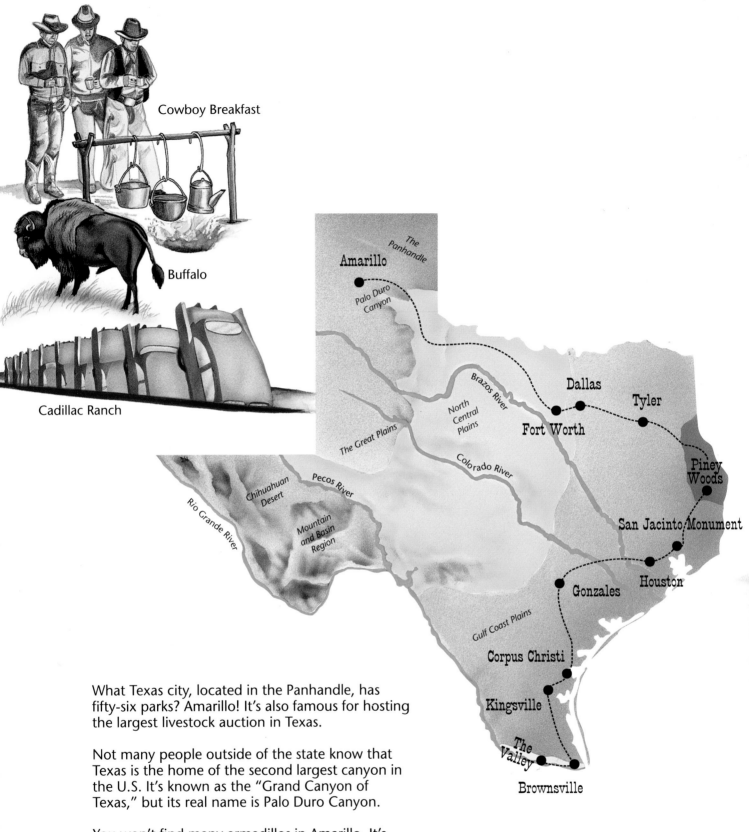

Cowboy Breakfast

Buffalo

Cadillac Ranch

The Panhandle

Amarillo

Palo Duro Canyon

The Great Plains

North Central Plains

Brazos River

Colorado River

Chihuahuan Desert

Pecos River

Rio Grande River

Mountain and Basin Region

Dallas

Fort Worth

Tyler

Piney Woods

San Jacinto Monument

Houston

Gonzales

Gulf Coast Plains

Corpus Christi

Kingsville

The Valley

Brownsville

What Texas city, located in the Panhandle, has fifty-six parks? Amarillo! It's also famous for hosting the largest livestock auction in Texas.

Not many people outside of the state know that Texas is the home of the second largest canyon in the U.S. It's known as the "Grand Canyon of Texas," but its real name is Palo Duro Canyon.

You won't find many armadillos in Amarillo. It's too cold. However, from time to time one does migrate as far north as the Panhandle.

We're headin' up north
To view Amarillo
Where cattle are plenty,
But not armadillo.

Hungry? Let's stop for
A barbecued steak.
How 'bout some chili,
Pecan pie, or fruitcake?

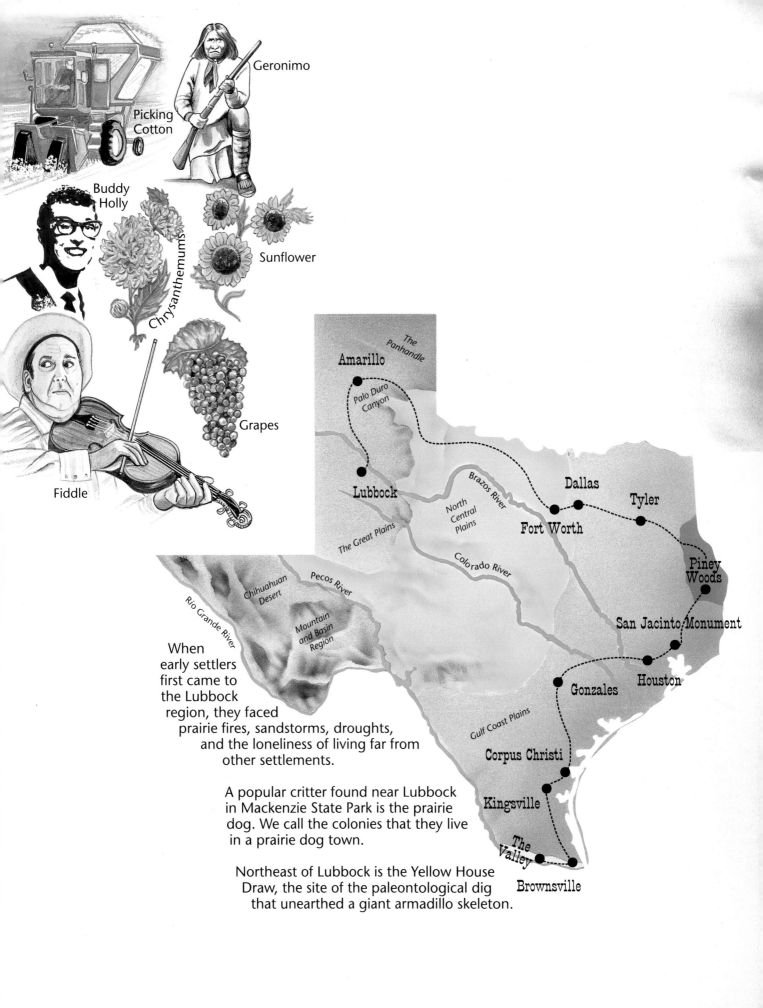

Picking Cotton

Geronimo

Buddy Holly

Chrysanthemums

Sunflower

Grapes

Fiddle

The Panhandle

Amarillo

Palo Duro Canyon

Lubbock

The Great Plains

Brazos River

North Central Plains

Colorado River

Dallas

Fort Worth

Tyler

Piney Woods

San Jacinto Monument

Houston

Gonzales

Rio Grande River

Chihuahuan Desert

Pecos River

Mountain and Basin Region

Gulf Coast Plains

Corpus Christi

Kingsville

The Valley

Brownsville

When early settlers first came to the Lubbock region, they faced prairie fires, sandstorms, droughts, and the loneliness of living far from other settlements.

A popular critter found near Lubbock in Mackenzie State Park is the prairie dog. We call the colonies that they live in a prairie dog town.

Northeast of Lubbock is the Yellow House Draw, the site of the paleontological dig that unearthed a giant armadillo skeleton.

On now to Lubbock,
Yee-ha, time to go.
Here prairie dogs pop up
From their homes down below.

On these Great Plains,
Not so long ago,
Indians once reigned
With the brown buffalo.

Today this flat land
Grows cotton in rows,
While the West Texas wind
Steadily blows.

Let's ride out west
To the town of El Paso,
Where tumbleweeds whirl
As swift as a lasso.

Through this great pass,
Came the brave pioneer,
Who faced many dangers
On the Texas frontier.

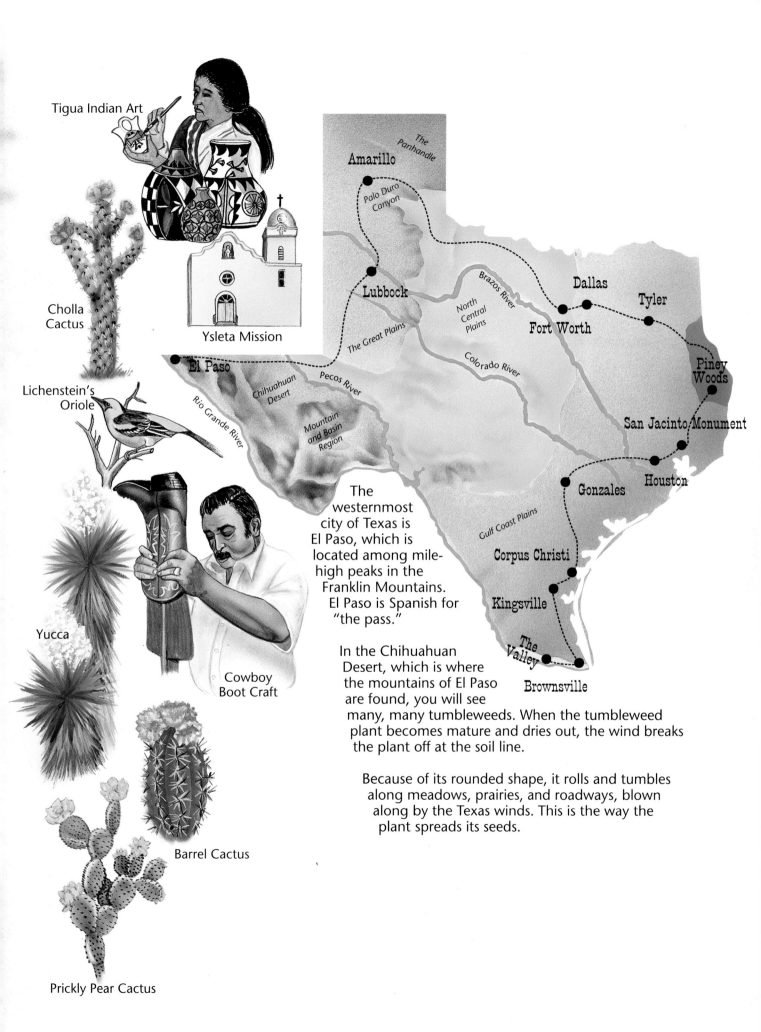

Tigua Indian Art

Cholla Cactus

Ysleta Mission

Lichenstein's Oriole

Yucca

Cowboy Boot Craft

Barrel Cactus

Prickly Pear Cactus

The Panhandle

Amarillo

Palo Duro Canyon

Lubbock

The Great Plains

Brazos River

North Central Plains

Dallas

Fort Worth

Tyler

Piney Woods

El Paso

Chihuahuan Desert

Pecos River

Rio Grande River

Mountain and Basin Region

Colorado River

San Jacinto Monument

Houston

Gonzales

Corpus Christi

Gulf Coast Plains

Kingsville

The Valley

Brownsville

The westernmost city of Texas is El Paso, which is located among mile-high peaks in the Franklin Mountains. El Paso is Spanish for "the pass."

In the Chihuahuan Desert, which is where the mountains of El Paso are found, you will see many, many tumbleweeds. When the tumbleweed plant becomes mature and dries out, the wind breaks the plant off at the soil line.

Because of its rounded shape, it rolls and tumbles along meadows, prairies, and roadways, blown along by the Texas winds. This is the way the plant spreads its seeds.

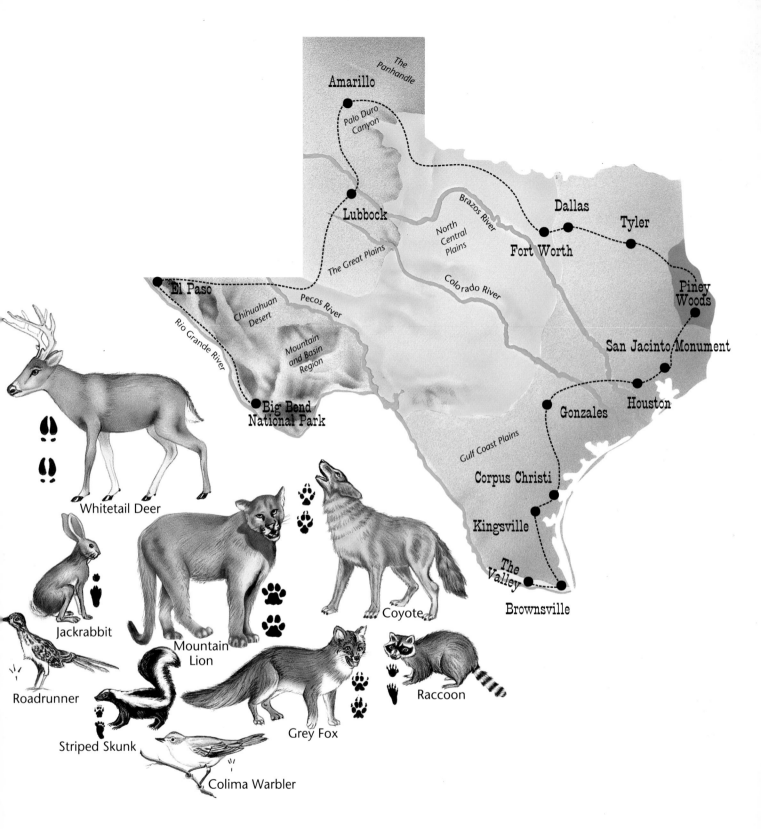

The Panhandle

Amarillo

Palo Duro Canyon

Lubbock

The Great Plains

Brazos River

North Central Plains

Dallas

Fort Worth

Tyler

Colorado River

El Paso

Chihuahuan Desert

Pecos River

Piney Woods

Rio Grande River

Mountain and Basin Region

San Jacinto Monument

Big Bend National Park

Houston

Gonzales

Gulf Coast Plains

Corpus Christi

Kingsville

The Valley

Brownsville

Whitetail Deer

Jackrabbit

Roadrunner

Mountain Lion

Coyote

Striped Skunk

Grey Fox

Raccoon

Colima Warbler

Big Bend National Park is located in West Texas on a gigantic bend in the Rio Grande River. A Native American legend explains that after creating Earth, the Great Spirit threw all the leftover rocks on the land of Big Bend. 99% of the park is desert. Do you know which desert?

In 1971, Douglas A. Lawson found the radius bone of a pterodactyl larger than any ever discovered before. Its wingspread is 51 feet!

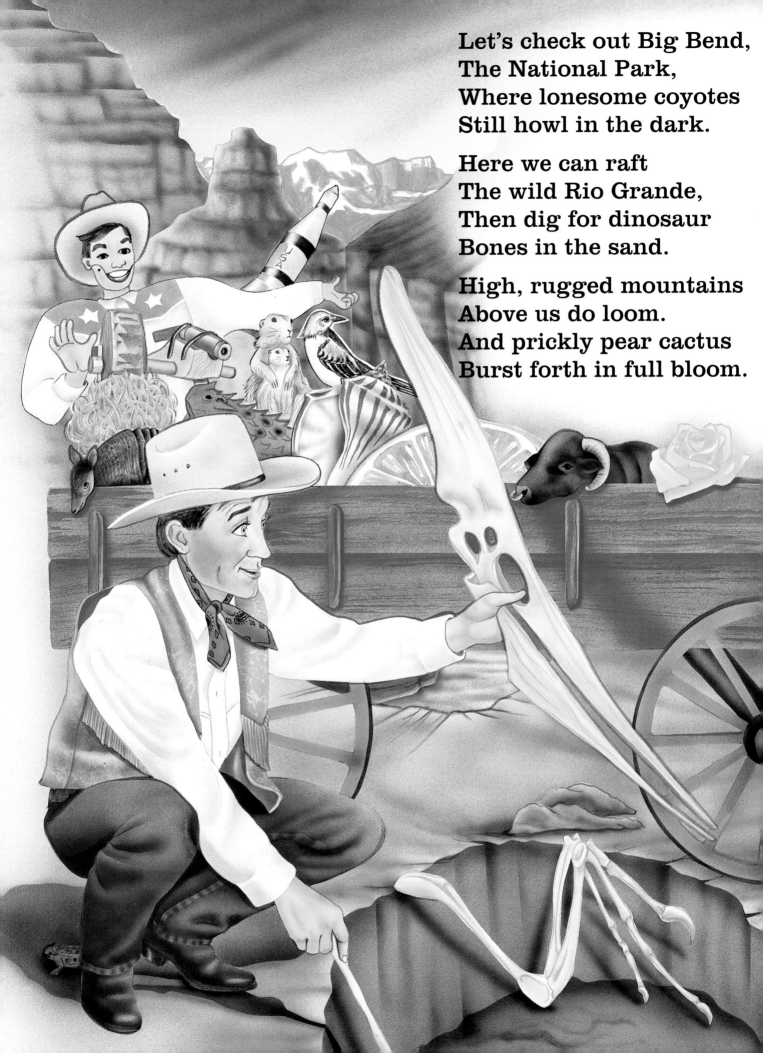

Let's check out Big Bend,
The National Park,
Where lonesome coyotes
Still howl in the dark.

Here we can raft
The wild Rio Grande,
Then dig for dinosaur
Bones in the sand.

High, rugged mountains
Above us do loom.
And prickly pear cactus
Burst forth in full bloom.

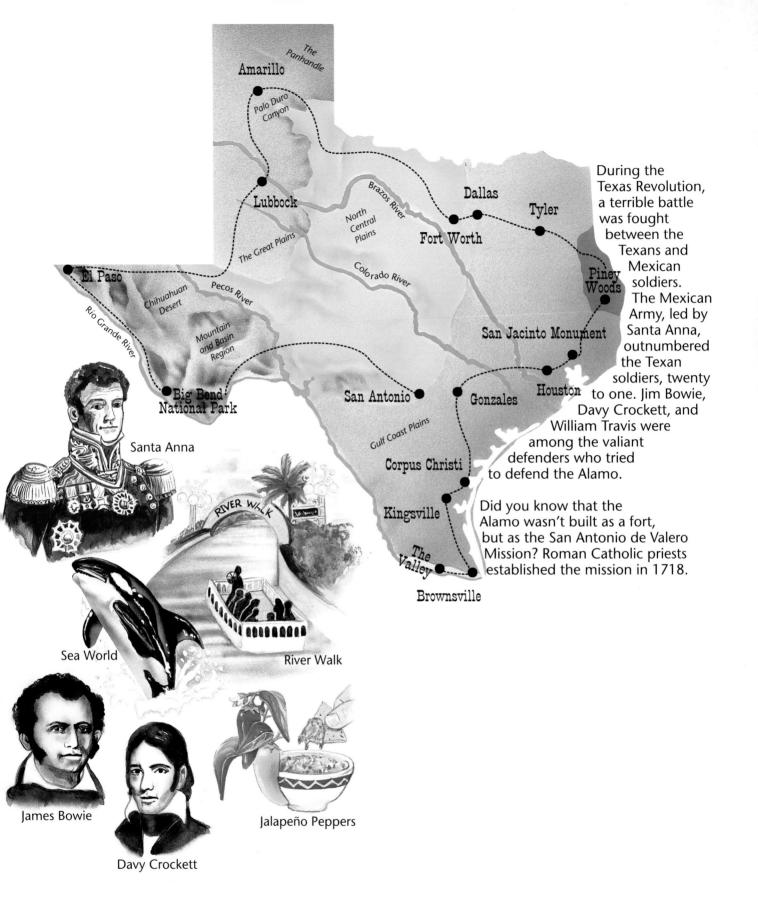

The Panhandle

Amarillo

Palo Duro Canyon

Lubbock

Brazos River

North Central Plains

Dallas

Tyler

Fort Worth

The Great Plains

El Paso

Colorado River

Piney Woods

Chihuahuan Desert

Pecos River

Rio Grande River

Mountain and Basin Region

San Jacinto Monument

Big Bend National Park

San Antonio

Gonzales

Houston

Santa Anna

Gulf Coast Plains

Corpus Christi

RIVER WALK

Kingsville

Sea World

River Walk

The Valley

Brownsville

James Bowie

Davy Crockett

Jalapeño Peppers

During the Texas Revolution, a terrible battle was fought between the Texans and Mexican soldiers. The Mexican Army, led by Santa Anna, outnumbered the Texan soldiers, twenty to one. Jim Bowie, Davy Crockett, and William Travis were among the valiant defenders who tried to defend the Alamo.

Did you know that the Alamo wasn't built as a fort, but as the San Antonio de Valero Mission? Roman Catholic priests established the mission in 1718.

San Antonio is next
Where we stroll the riverwalk.
Here many people dine
While others sit and talk.

Let's wander on over
To the old Alamo,
Where Texas bluebonnets
Sway to and fro.

The Alamo soldiers
Were so brave and grand.
They fought for our Texas
By taking a stand.

Pardners, we're now at
The end of our trail,
In Hill Country's Austin,
Where longhorns prevail.

Austin's the capital
Of our Lone Star State.
See the flag waving?
Isn't it great?